Dealing With

MY PARENTS'
DIVORCE

by Jane Lacey
Illustrated by Venitia Dean

W
FRANKLIN WATTS

Franklin Watts
Published in paperback in Great Britain in 2019 by The Watts Publishing Group

Copyright © The Watts Publishing Group, 2017
The text in this book was originally published in the series 'How can I deal with'

Credits
Series Editor: Sarah Peutrill
Series Design: Collaborate

Every attempt has been made to clear copyright. Should there be any
inadvertent omission please apply to the publisher for rectification.

ISBN 978 1 4451 5792 4

Printed in China

Franklin Watts
An imprint of
Hachette Children's Group
Part of The Watts Publishing Group
Carmelite House
50 Victoria Embankment
London EC4Y 0DZ

An Hachette UK Company
www.hachette.co.uk

www.franklinwatts.co.uk

Contents

My home isn't a happy place to be any more 4

What is divorce or separation? 8

My parents are getting a divorce 9

I feel angry with my mum and dad 12

Is my parents' divorce my fault? 15

What's going to happen to me? 18

I'm ashamed about my parents' divorce 22

How can I love both my mum and dad? 24

Will we be happy again? 27

It happened to us: playscript 28

Glossary 30

Further information 31

Notes for parents, carers and teachers 32

Index 32

MY HOME ISN'T A HAPPY PLACE TO BE ANY MORE

Holly's mum and dad argue a lot. They never seem to smile or laugh or have fun. Holly's home isn't as happy as it used to be.

Luli is Holly's friend

Holly's my best friend but she never asks me round to her house. She always wants to come home with me. She says she wishes my mum and dad were her mum and dad.

Luli

4

Holly's story

Mum and Dad keep shouting at each other. Sometimes they just don't talk.

If I want a chat or a story or a hug they say, "Go away, Holly! Not now, Holly! Later, Holly."

They never have time for me.

My friend Luli's mum and dad are always smiling.

When I go round to play they say, "Hello, Holly. Lovely to see you."

They take us swimming and we go to the park. Luli's mum cooks delicious food. We laugh and have fun.

5

What can Holly do?

She can:

* ★ try to talk to her mum and dad when they aren't arguing or busy
* ★ tell them how she feels - that she wishes they had more time to spend with her and she wants them all to have fun together.

What Holly did

I talked to Mum and Dad. They said sorry. They said they made each other unhappy, but they did not want to make me unhappy, too. Luli came round and Mum took us to the park. We had spaghetti bolognese for tea. My favourite!

I think Mum and Dad are going to get a divorce.

It helps to talk to your mum or dad.

Before my husband and I got divorced, we were very unhappy. We were too busy arguing to notice that our son Chris was unhappy, too.

So when Chris told us that he wanted to leave home and live with his grandparents, we were shocked!

But we were glad Chris told us how he was feeling. It meant we could help him to feel better. We tried not to argue in front of Chris. We made sure we still had happy times with him.

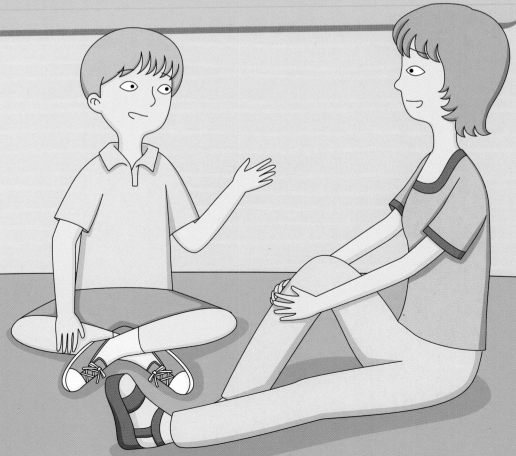

WHAT IS DIVORCE OR SEPARATION?

Parents split up, or separate, when they decide not to live together any more. If they are married, they can get a divorce. They sign papers that make them single again.

After parents split up, children usually live with either their mum or their dad and visit the one they are not living with. A judge may help to make sure this is fair.

Parents split up from each other, not their children. They will always be their children's mum and dad. It is never the children's fault.

MY PARENTS ARE GETTING A DIVORCE

Billy knows his parents are getting a divorce, but he doesn't understand what it means. It makes him feel worried and afraid.

Billy's story

Mum and Dad are getting a divorce but they didn't tell me much about it. My friend Joe's parents got divorced, but I haven't asked him about it. I'm afraid divorce means something bad will happen.

what can Billy do?

He can:

★ ask his parents to tell him what divorce means
★ say he is worried about what will happen
★ talk to his friend Joe.

What Billy did

I asked Mum and Dad what divorce meant and they explained. They said they would make sure I agreed about what happened to me.

I talked to my friend Joe. He told me that things had worked out all right for him. I feel better now about what's going to happen.

Joe is Billy's friend

When my mum and dad got divorced, Dad moved out and I stayed with Mum.

I see Dad nearly every Sunday and we go out together. We talk on the phone or email almost every day.

He's buying a flat so I'll be able to stay with him soon. We're going away together on holiday in the summer.

Mum works and sometimes Gran collects me from school and gives me tea. Things have changed but it's OK. It's not as bad as I thought it was going to be.

Dad and I still have fun.

I FEEL ANGRY WITH MY MUM AND DAD

Gracie's parents are splitting up. She feels angry with them for letting it happen. She thinks they should try harder to get on with each other.

Gracie

Gracie's story

I feel really cross with Mum and Dad. They are going to split up and they are spoiling everything!

When my sister and I argue, they tell us to say sorry and be friends! Why can't they do the same?

What can Gracie do?

She can:

★ tell her parents how she feels about the separation - that she is angry with them and that they should make up
★ listen to what her parents say.

What Gracie did

I told Mum and Dad they were spoiling everything. I said, "Why do you have to split up?"

They said they had tried hard to work things out.

They were sad they were splitting up. I don't feel so angry with Mum and Dad any more.

At least that will make them happy!

Alfie was also angry when his mum and dad split up.

Alfie's Story

Last year, my dad left my mum, me and my little sister and went to live with his girlfriend. I was really angry.

Now my little sister and I are supposed to visit Dad every other weekend. I wouldn't go at first. I was so angry with Dad. He shouldn't have left us!

But Mum said she wanted me and Dad to be friends. Now Dad and I have tennis lessons together. We went to the beach last weekend. We have a nice time, but I still haven't been to his new home. Maybe I will soon.

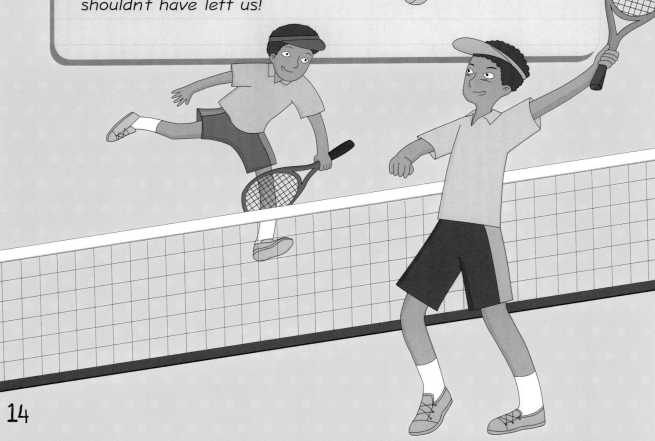

IS MY PARENTS' DIVORCE MY FAULT?

Rosa worries that it's her fault her parents are getting a divorce. She thinks she can stop it happening by always being kind and good.

Mo   Rosa

Mo is Rosa's friend

Rosa and I used to have lots of fun. Sometimes we were quite naughty and got the giggles.

But she's changed. She never wants to be naughty. She even worries about little things like getting her clothes dirty or making a spelling mistake. I don't know what's the matter with her!

I haven't told anyone, but Mum and Dad are splitting up. Dad's going to leave home.

Sometimes I can be really naughty. I'm worried that it's my fault they are splitting up. I want to make things better so Mum and Dad will be happy together again. I make them cards and presents, I tidy my room, I work hard at school. I don't argue with my younger brother and sister.

I think that if I'm very good, maybe they won't get divorced and Dad will stay with us.

16

what can Rosa do?

She can:

* ★ talk to someone she trusts, such as her friend Mo, her grandparents or her teacher
* ★ remember that her parents' divorce is not her fault
* ★ tell her parents how she feels.

what Rosa did

I talked to my friend Mo. She said when her mum and dad got a divorce, they told her it wasn't her fault. She said it's not my fault either.

There's nothing I can do to make my mum and dad stay together. I wish there was, but at least I don't have to be good all the time, after all!

WHAT'S GOING TO HAPPEN TO ME?

Ed is worried about what is going to happen to him when his parents split up. He thinks everything will change. He doesn't think any of the changes will be good ones.

Sangita is Ed's friend

Ed thinks we won't be friends after his mum and dad split up.

He's worried he'll have to move house and go to a different school.

But I think we can always be friends, whatever happens.

Ed's story

I know my mum and dad are splitting up but I don't know what's going to happen to me.

Where will I live and who will I live with - Mum or Dad?

If we have to move, will my new home be as nice as this one?

Will we have enough money?

Will I have to change school?

Can I still play in the football team?

Will I lose all my friends?

Will I still see Gran and Granddad?

I'm worried about everything!

19

What can Ed do?

He can:

★ talk to his mum and dad about his worries - things might not be as bad as he thinks

★ talk to his friends and make plans to keep in touch - they can talk on the phone, email and visit each other.

What Ed did

I asked Mum and Dad what was going to happen. They said we were going to sell our house but they didn't know where my new home would be.

They said, if I did change school I would make new friends. They've promised to help me keep in touch with my old friends and play football. I'll still see Gran and Granddad.

Sometimes, parents who are separating or getting a divorce can't agree on what to do about money and their children. When that happens, a mediator can help.

A mediator's story

An important part of my job is to listen. I listen to both parents and I listen to the children. I help them all to listen to each other.

They all say what they want to happen and what they think is fair.

I help them to make the best plan they can, even if it isn't perfect.

I'M ASHAMED ABOUT MY PARENTS' DIVORCE

Louis feels ashamed. He does not want his friends to find out that his parents are divorced.

Louis's story

Louis

I don't want my friends to know what has happened at home. I pretend Dad is still living with us. I don't ask my friends round to my house in case they find out he's gone.

I flew my kite with my friend yesterday. I pretended I was happy and I didn't tell her what is happening. I feel ashamed my family don't live together any more.

Louis's teacher's story

Louis should not be ashamed at all. About one in four children in the country have parents who have split up, so he isn't the only one. It has happened to several other children in my class and no one thinks the worse of them.

He can talk to me about it. He can talk to one of the other children whose parents are divorced.

Keeping a secret can make you feel unhappy. It can really help to talk about what is happening to you.

23

HOW CAN I LOVE BOTH MY MUM AND DAD?

Now Darcy lives with her mum and just visits her dad, she worries that she won't be able to love them both the same.

Lily is Darcy's friend

Darcy lives next door. I play with her after school and at weekends.

She keeps worrying about her dad. She thinks she should keep him company and not be having fun here with me.

Lily

Darcy's story

After Mum and Dad split up, Dad went to live in a flat. My sister and I, the dog and cat live with Mum.

I think Dad is lonely and misses us all. I feel bad when I'm having fun as he is on his own. I think I should be with him to cheer him up and keep him company.

But if I lived with Dad, then Mum and my sister would miss me. I'd miss them too.

I don't know what to do.
I want everyone to be happy!

Darcy

She can:

* chat to her dad on the phone and tell him her news
* send him emails, letters, pictures and photos that will make him smile
* ask her dad to do the same for her.

what Darcy did

Sometimes I ring Dad and sometimes he rings me for a chat. He says my pictures and letters cheer him up. He tells me nice things he is doing so I don't worry about him.

When I visit, I sometimes take our dog Buster, and we all go for a walk.

WILL WE BE HAPPY AGAIN?

When parents split up, it can be upsetting for everyone in the family. But things usually work out for everyone in the end.

Fred's story

When Mum and Dad split up, all the family were upset. I didn't think I'd ever be happy again! I thought I wouldn't see Mum after she moved out. I thought Dad wouldn't be any good at looking after us.

But I see Mum lots and we send emails every day too. Dad isn't such a bad cook after all! I know Mum will always be my mum and Dad will always be my dad and they'll always love me, whatever happens.

IT HAPPENED TO US

Henry and Ally's parents' divorce was very upsetting, but now everything is much better.

Henry and Ally's story

Henry: One day, my sister Ally and I had a big fight, I can't remember why.

Ally: Dad really shouted at us. Then Mum shouted at us. Then Dad and Mum had a row.

Henry: I said to Ally, "Do you think Mum and Dad are going to split up?"

Ally: I said, "If they do, it's our fault because we're naughty and we keep fighting!"

Henry: But Mum and Dad said, "It's not your fault we're getting a divorce."

Ally: We stopped fighting and being naughty, but it didn't make any difference.

Henry: Mum and Dad got a divorce anyway. We were really worried and unhappy. We didn't want things to change.

Ally: We moved to a smaller house but we stayed at the same school. Dad moved out but he didn't go far away.

Henry: We chat to Dad on the phone or email him nearly every day. We have fun when we stay with him.

Ally: We have got new partners now and they've got children. Now we're part of a really big family!

Henry: Things have worked out okay. It's much better than we thought it would be.

GLOSSARY

Ashamed
When you feel ashamed you are embarrassed. You don't want anyone to know something about you so you keep it a secret.

Divorce
Divorce is when a husband and wife sign legal papers that mean they are not married any more.

Fault
If something is your fault, it means you have caused something bad to happen.

Feelings
Feelings are the way you feel about what is happening to you. You can feel happy or sad, brave or afraid, bored or excited.

Married
Two people are married when they sign papers that make them husband and wife.

Mediator
A mediator helps people who disagree to find a way to agree and make plans for the future.

Separate
Parents separate when they decide not to live together any more and, if they are married, to get a divorce.

Single
Someone who is single isn't married. When parents get divorced, they become single again.

Splitting up
Parents split up when they decide not to live together any more and, if they are married, to get a divorce.

Trust
When you trust someone, you know they will tell you the truth and look after you.

Worry
You worry when you don't know what is going to happen and you think of all the bad things that might happen.

Further information

For children

www.childline.org.uk
Tel: 0800 1111
Childline is a free helpline for children in the UK. You can talk to someone about any problem and they will help you to sort it out.

kidshealth.org
Check out the feelings section to learn more about divorce.

For readers in Australia and New Zealand

kidshelpline.com.au
Tel: 1800 55 1800
Kidshelp is the free helpline for children in Australia. You can talk to someone about any problem.

www.cyh.com
Loads of online information about all sorts of issues, including parents who are splitting up.

www.kidsline.org.nz
A helpline run by specially trained young volunteers to help kids and teens deal with troubling issues and problems.

For parents

www.familylives.org.uk
Helpline for parents:
0808 800 2222
The Family Lives charity offers advice, guidance and support for parents who are concerned about their children.

www.gingerbread.org.uk
Gingerbread provides expert advice, practical support and campaigns for single parents.

Note to parents and teachers: Every effort has been made by the Publishers to ensure these websites are suitable for children, that they are of the highest educational standard and that they contain no inappropriate or offensive material. However, because of the nature of the Internet, it is impossible to guarantee that the contents of these sites will not be altered. We strongly advise that Internet access is supervised by a responsible adult.

INDEX

arguments 4, 5, 6, 7, 12, 16, 28

feeling
  angry 12–13, 14
  ashamed 22–23, 30
  unhappy 4–5, 6, 7, 23, 27, 28-29
  worried 9, 10, 15, 16, 18–19, 24–25, 29, 30

is it my fault? 8, 15, 16, 17, 28

keeping in touch 11, 14, 20, 26, 27, 29

mediator 21, 30

talking about it 6–7, 10, 13, 17, 20, 23

what is divorce? 8–9, 10, 30

what will happen? 18–19, 20, 27, 29

Notes for parents, carers and teachers

When parents separate or divorce, children will be affected. There are many ways that parents, carers and teachers can help children to deal with their parents' divorce and make it as easy for them as possible.

- Children need to know that their parents' divorce is not their fault
- It helps to have an adult they trust to listen to them and to take their worries seriously
- Parents can help by not involving children in arguments or asking them to take sides
- Keeping up routines and discipline can help children to feel safe.

Page 5 Holly's story

Holly's parents are too busy with their own problems to notice that Holly feels unhappy and left out.

- Reassurance and love can help children to get through a difficult time.

Page 9 Billy's story

Billy doesn't know what divorce means and he is thinking the worst.

- Telling children what is going on will help them to understand and not be afraid.

Page 12 Gracie's story

Gracie is angry with her parents for not making things work.

- Knowing that their parents have tried their best can help children not to be so angry.

Page 16 Rosa's story

Rosa thinks her parents' divorce is her fault. She wants to make things better

- Divorce is never the children's fault. It's not up to them to make it all right and they need to be told this.

Page 19 Ed's story

Ed is worried and afraid that things will be worse for him after the divorce.

- Involving children in plans and keeping them informed will help them not to worry. Things are usually not as bad as they fear.

Page 22 Louis's story

Louis is embarrassed and ashamed about his dad leaving home.

- Secrets can make children feel unhappy. Talking to an adult they trust will help them to know that other children are going through the same experience.

Page 25 Darcy's story

Darcy feels responsible for making her parents happy.

- Children are not responsible for their parents' happiness. Parents can discuss ways to have a good time with their children and make sure they happen even when they are arguing themselves.

Page 28 Playscript, Henry and Ally's story

Children could perform the parts in this simple playscript. It's an opportunity to reinforce the point that divorce is never the children's fault. They could also write and perform their own play about divorce.